Catch up Level 9

Dream Team

David Bennett

D1826531

Oxford University Press

Dream Team

The Cast

Mr Slater, the team leader, aged about 45

Miss Green, also a teacher, aged about 35

Adam
Gary
Clair } all aged 14-15
Sally

Scene 1

(Outside the Catbells Outdoor Pursuit Centre in Cumbria. Friday night, 6.30 p.m.)

Mr Slater: *(Keenly)* Here we are at last, the Catbells Outdoor Pursuit Centre. This will be our home for the next week.

Adam: *(Miserably)* It looks a right dump, Sir.

Gary: Yes, Sir, a right flea pit.

Mr Slater: *(Breathing in)* Oh come on Dream Team. Let's be keen! Take a deep breath just smell that air. Real fresh air! So pure! And look at the Outdoor Centre. It's built in real Cumbrian slate.

Adam: With real Cumbrian holes!

Sally: Shut up Adam and stop moaning.

Miss Green: You had better get used to it, Sally. He will be doing it all week.

Gary: I must be mad giving up my holiday for a week's walking in the hills.

Adam: I could be in my nice warm bed.

Sally: Cuddling your teddy!

Gary: No Sally, you're wrong it's not his teddy. Adam is grown up now. He's into Barbies!

Adam: Get lost. Just because you like Cindy!

Mr Slater: *(Keenly)* Just look at those hills. I can't wait to get started tomorrow. Fresh air, plenty of excercise and the best drinking water in the world!

Clair: Where, Sir?

Mr Slater: In the mountain streams, Clair. *(Dreamily)* In the mountain streams.

Miss Green: What better way to spend half-term?

Adam: In bed, Miss!

Miss Green: Now I hope you are not going to moan all week, Adam Hodgson.

Adam: Yes, Miss… er… I mean no, Miss.

Mr Slater: *(Keenly)* Right team. Action stations. Gary, you and Sally make up the beds. Adam, you and Clair sort out the food.

Adam: And what are you and Miss Green going to do, Sir? Have a rest?

Mr Slater: *(Seriously)* We will be planning tomorrow's walk.

Adam: *(Laughing)* As I said, Sir. Having a rest!

Scene 2

*(In Girls' Room. **Gary** and **Sally** are making up the beds.)*

Gary: These beds are hard. I think they must be made of that Cumbrian Slate.

Sally: Don't you start. One moaner like Adam is enough.

Gary: Yes, sorry. He's a pain, isn't he?

Sally: This week will sort him out.

Gary: Yeah. I can't wait to see him half-way up a rock face.

Sally: You can bet your life he will still be moaning.

Gary: Oh I know! Adam would moan if he won ten million on the lottery. It wouldn't be enough. Why have you come on this week, Sal?

Sally: My dad really. Things have been a bit bad at home since mum left... What about you, Gary. What made you come?

Gary: Angie dumped me two weeks ago. So I said I'd come on the trip. I thought it would help take my mind off her. Then, last week we got back together again but it was too late to get out of this trip. I'm missing her already!

Sally: You big softy! Never mind we'll soon be back home. What are we doing tomorrow?

Gary: Walking the Catbells Ridge, so Slater says. He makes me laugh. *(Speaking like* **Mr Slater***)* 'Just smell that air, team. Real fresh air.'

Sally: His heart's in the right place.

Gary: True.

Mr Slater: *(Shouting)* You two finished up there yet?

Sally: Nearly, Sir.

Mr Slater: *(Keenly)* Hurry up then. I can't wait to show you tomorrow's route.

Scene 3

*(In the kitchen. **Adam** and **Clair** are unpacking food.)*

Clair: Are you looking forward to this week, Adam?

Adam: No.

Clair: Oh! So why are you here then?

Adam: *(Seriously)* It's my guinea pig's fault.

Clair: Your guinea pig?

Adam: *(Very seriously)* Yes. It died.

Clair: *(Amazed)* What has that got to do with you coming on this trip?

Adam: My mum wants me to bury it where she found it.

Clair: And where was that?

Adam: The Catbells Ridge!

Clair: You mean you have brought a dead guinea pig with you?

Adam: Yes. It's in my rucksack!

Clair: You're joking?

Adam: *(Smiling)* Yes, you're right, I'm joking. Why are you here then?

Clair: I like walking in the mountains.

Adam: *(Amazed)* You like walking?

Clair: Yes.

Adam: There are some strange people about!

Mr Slater: *(Shouting)* Are you two ready yet? I want to show you what we're doing tomorrow.

Clair/Adam: *(Together)* Coming, Sir.

Scene 4

(In the living room. All the team are looking at a map.)

Mr Slater: Right team, listen carefully. Tomorrow we shall be tackling the Catbells Ridge. This is a four-mile walk. In full gear. Big boots, ropes, the works. It will be hard. Very hard.

Miss Green: *(Getting excited)* But the views are super. Really super. We will be alone. Just us and the mountains. Us against nature. Who will win I wonder?

Gary: You make it sound like we are going up Everest, Miss.

Miss Green: It will be like that, Gary!

Mr Slater: Right then. Time for bed. A good night's sleep is what we all need.

Sally: *(Amazed)* But it's only eight-thirty, Sir!

Mr Slater: Exactly, Sally. No time to waste. We don't want to be tired out in the morning, do we?

Adam: But Sir.

Miss Green: I thought you liked your bed, Adam!

Adam: Not that much, Miss!

Mr Slater: Come on Dream Team time for bed. Breakfast is at 0600 hours, sharp.

All: *(Groaning)* Yes, Sir.

Scene 5

(The foot of the Catbells Ridge. Saturday 8.30 a.m.)

Gary: *(Pointing upwards)* Is that it, Sir?

Mr Slater: That is it team. The Catbells Ridge.

Sally: It doesn't look very high, Sir.

Adam: *(Moaning)* It looks high enough to me. Have we got to go all the way up there, Sir?

Mr Slater: Right to the top, Adam. Right to the top.

Gary: *(Pointing)* What's that up there, Sir?

MrSlater: *(Looking up)* Where, Gary?

Gary: About half-way up the ridge, Sir.

Clair: Oh yes. I see it. It looks like a baby's buggy.

Miss Green: And if I'm not mistaken, it has a baby in it.

Clair: You're never wrong, Miss, and it has got a baby in it.

Gary: If a baby can get to the top, then so can we.

Mr Slater: Never mind the baby Dream Team, it's time for some serious mountain climbing.

Gary: But it's just a walk up there, Sir. Look that lady is doing it pushing a buggy.

Mr Slater: We're taking no chances Gary. Boots on and ropes out team.

Adam: My boots are killing me.

Sally: *(Startled)* But you haven't even got them on yet.

Adam: It's the thought of putting them on that's killing me.

Mr Slater: Okay, Dream Team, I'll go first then Gary, Sally, Adam, Clair, and finally Miss Green. No slacking now. Follow me.

Gary: *(Moaning)* Look at us. Ropes, big boots, the works and it's only a little hill we're going up.

Sally: Yes, it's a bit over the top, isn't it?

Gary: I wish we were.

Sally: You wish we were what?

Gary: Over the top.

Sally: Why?

Gary: *(Laughing)* Then we'd be going downhill!

Sally: You went downhill a long time ago, Gary!

Mr Slater: I think we'll have a rest here.

Clair: But we've only gone 500 metres sir!

Mr Slater: All good walkers know when to rest, Clair.

Adam: All old men know when to rest more like!

Miss Green: No. Mr Slater is right, Adam. We need to rest.

Gary: After 500 metres Miss?

Miss Green: Yes, Gary. We must save our energy for the rest of the day.

Sally: At this rate it will take us all week to do this one walk.

Mr Slater: Ten minutes stop here Dream Team. We will set off again at 09.00.

Scene 6

(The team are resting 500 metres up the Catbells Ridge.)

Gary: I don't believe it.

Adam: What?

Clair: *(Looking around)* Who? What? Why? Where?

Gary: Getting out of that bus.

Adam: What?

Gary: Those men and women.

Adam: So?

Gary: They're coming up here onto Catbells.

Adam: So?

Sally: Just look at what they are wearing.

Mr Slater: *(Worriedly)* Oh dear. Oh dear. They should not be coming up here dressed like that. Not in skirts and high heels.

Adam: And that's just the men, Sir!

Miss Green: No Adam, seriously. You need the right equipment to go up mountains.

Adam: Whatever they're wearing, they're coming this way.

Clair: Let's go before they catch us up.

Mr Slater: *(Firmly)* Not yet Clair, 09.00 is our restart time.

Adam: But Sir, we don't want a load of old codgers going past us.

Gary: How come they aren't roped up like us?

Mr Slater: *(Shaking his head)* They should be, Gary. They should be.

Adam: *(Joking)* They look fifty times older than us, Sir. That's nearly as old as you.

Miss Green: Oh Adam, don't be so rotten. Mr Slater is a young man.

Adam: You might think fifty-two is young, Miss. I don't.

Miss Green: Adam Hodgson, Mr Slater is only… well it doesn't matter how old he is.

Sally: Here they come.

Gary: *(Cheerfully)* Good morning.

Sally: *(Cheerfully)* Good morning.

Adam: *(Miserably)* Morning.

Mr Slater: *(Very keenly)* A very good morning to you. Lovely to be out in the fresh air.

Miss Green: Wonderful, wonderful day.

Adam: Look at that. Not one of them spoke to me.

Sally: I would have thought you would know why.

Adam: Why?

Sally: *(Laughing)* Well who, in their right mind, would talk to a fifteen year-old boy who has a Barbie doll sticking out of his rucksac?

Adam: I haven't... have I?

All: Yes!

Mr Slater: *(Rapping)* 09.00 Dream Team. Let's be mean and live our dream!

Adam: Mad or what?

Clair: Mad!

Scene 7

(Close to the top of Catbells. Saturday, 11 a.m.)

Adam: How much further is it, Sir? My feet are killing me.

Mr Slater: Just over the top of this hill, Adam, and we will be there.

Sally: You said that ten minutes ago.

Clair: And ten minutes before that!

Gary: And twenty minutes before that!

Miss Green: Oh come on boys and girls if Mr Slater says it is over the next hill, then it will be over the next hill. He is never wrong.

Adam: He is never right!

Mr Slater: There you are, see!

Gary: Where? Where?

Mr Slater: Just to the left about 250 metres ahead. The top of Catbells.

Sally: What is that there, Miss?

Miss Green: Where, Sally?

Sally: About 100 metres below the summit and a little to the left.

Mr Slater: It looks like the buggy that we saw earlier.

Miss Green: Yes, it does but I can't see the woman who was pushing it.

Clair: Listen.

Adam: I can't hear anything.

Clair: *(Loudly)* Shut up and listen, Adam.

Mr Slater: Quiet everybody

Adam: *(Bored)* Yes quiet, we want to listen to the wind.

Gary: In that case we could listen to you.

Adam: Why?

Gary: You're full of it.

Mr Slater: *(Shouting)* Quiet.

Clair: There did you hear it? A baby crying.

Miss Green: *(Worriedly)* Yes. Yes, I heard it. It is a baby crying.

Mr Slater: Okay, everybody, let's go and see just what is going on up there.

Adam: It's only a baby crying, Sir. It's probably dropped its dummy.

Gary: I wish we could drop our dummy.

Adam: What?

All: You!

Mr Slater: *(Rapping)* Come on Dream Team. Let's be mean and inspect the scene!

Scene 8

(The team have reached the baby in the buggy.)

Clair: *(Looking around)* I can't see her mother anywhere.

Sally: Where could she have gone?

Miss Green: Let's look at this sensibly. She didn't pass us as we were getting up here. So she must still be up here somewhere.

Adam: Brilliant, Miss. Watch out Sherlock Holmes is all I can say.

Gary: Well shut up then. This is serious. A mother doesn't leave her baby up here for no reason.

Mr Slater: We need to search the area, Dream Team. Adam and Miss Green take the left-hand side.

Adam: Yes, Sir.

Mr Slater: Sally you and Gary carry on up the path and ask those old people if they've seen anything.

Gary: On our way, Sir.

Mr Slater: Clair, you stay with the baby and I will search down the right-hand side of the ridge. If any of you see anything, give one long blast on your whistle and no more.

(The group split up and start their search.)

Adam: *(Picking up a shoe)* What's this?

Miss Green: It's one of her shoes. She was wearing red stiletto shoes. Don't you remember?

Adam: *(Smiling)* I wasn't looking at her feet, Miss.

Miss Green: Well, she was. I remember thinking at the time how silly they were for walking in.

Adam: *(Pointing)* You don't think she is down there do you, Miss?

Miss Green: There is only one way to find out Adam.

(They walk to the edge of the ridge and look over.)

Adam: *(Pointing)* There she is. Shall I go down?

Miss Green: No, Adam. It's best to wait for Mr Slater. Blow your whistle.

Scene 9

(On top of Catbells Ridge. Saturday, 12 noon. Mr Slater has climbed down to the woman.)

Mr Slater: *(Shouting up)* Okay, Dream Team she has been knocked out but she is alive. She needs help quickly.

Gary: Time to put what you have taught us into practice, Mr Slater.

Clair: Let's go.

Adam: *(Puzzled)* What are you on about?

Clair: You wouldn't know because you never listen.

Sally: Just do as you are told.

Mr Slater: Gary climb down here to me and bring the emergency gear. Miss Green will hold your rope.

(Gary *climbs down the edge.)*

Gary: Okay, I'm down.

Miss Green: Right. Sally, Clair, and Adam, you come with me.

Adam: Where are we going, Miss?

Miss Green: Off the mountain with the baby and to phone the Mountain Rescue. Mr Slater and Gary will stay up here with the lady.

(They start off down the mountain.)

Mr Slater: I don't want to move her. She might have hurt her spine. But we must keep her warm.

Gary: I'll get out the emergency blanket and sleeping bag. We could put them over her.

Mr Slater: Let's do it.

Gary: How long do you think she has been out cold?

Mr Slater: I have no idea but she needs help soon. Let's get her warm and wait for the rescue people.

Scene 10

(The kitchen of the Catbells Centre. Saturday, 8.30 p.m. **Mr Slater** *and* **Gary** *walk in.)*

Sally: Is she okay, Sir?

Mr Slater: Yes. She has had a lucky escape.

Clair: What happened?

Gary: She tripped on those silly shoes and fell over the edge.

Sally: It's lucky it wasn't a big drop.

Gary: A broken leg, a few cuts, and a sore head, that's all. They are keeping her in overnight.

Miss Green: The hospital are looking after the baby too. So all is well.

Adam: *(Pretending to be* **Mr Slater***)* You see Dream Team. If you respect the mountains, they will respect you. In fact, *(***Adam** *starts to rap)* If you show no fear, have the right gear, and take great care, then you can enjoy the fresh air.

Mr Slater: *(Laughing)* Come on Dream Team. We did a good job today but now it's time for bed.

Adam: But Sir, it's only eight-thirty.

Mr Slater: *(Slowly)* Exactly Adam, exactly!

OXFORD
UNIVERSITY PRESS

Great Clarendon Street, Oxford, OX2 6DP

Oxford University Press is a department of the University of Oxford.
It furthers the University's objective of excellence in research, scholarship,
and education by publishing worldwide in

Oxford New York

Athens Auckland Bangkok Bogotá Buenos Aires Calcutta
Cape Town Chennai Dar es Salaam Delhi Florence Hong Kong Istanbul
Karachi Kuala Lumpur Madrid Melbourne Mexico City Mumbai
Nairobi Paris São Paulo Shanghai Singapore Taipei Tokyo Toronto Warsaw

with associated companies in Berlin Ibadan

Oxford is a trade mark of Oxford University Press
in the UK and in certain other countries

First published 1998

Reprinted 2000

ISBN 0 19 833754 X

Printed in Great Britain

Illustrations by Chris Molan